THE STORY OF THE GOLDEN STATE WARRIORS

Chris Mullin

MULLIN

17

Klay Thompson

A HISTORY OF HOOPS

THE STORY OF THE

GOLDEN STATE WARRIORS

JIM WHITING

Tim Hardaway

CREATIVE EDUCATION / CREATIVE PAPERBACKS

Published by Creative Education and Creative Paperbacks
P.O. Box 227, Mankato, Minnesota 56002
Creative Education and Creative Paperbacks are imprints of
The Creative Company
www.thecreativecompany.us

Design and production by Blue Design (www.bluedes.com)
Art direction by Rita Marshall
Production layout by Rachel Klimpel and Ciara Beitlich

Photographs by AP Images (Jeff Chiu, Jed Jacobsohn, Al Messerschmidt
Archive, Ezra Shaw, Paul Vathis, Nick Wass), Getty (Andrew D. Bernstein,
Focus On Sport, Otto Greule Jr., Thearon W. Henderson, Bob Levey, John
W. McDonough, NBA Photos, Pool, Dick Raphael, San Francisco Chronicle/
Hearst Newspapers, Ezra Shaw, Rocky Widner), Shutterstock (Brocreative),
Twitter (Justin Kubatko), Wikimedia Commons (The Sporting News Archives)

Library of Congress Cataloging-in-Publication Data
Names: Whiting, Jim, 1943- author.
Title: The story of the Golden State Warriors / by Jim Whiting.
Description: Mankato, Minnesota : Creative Education/Creative
    Paperbacks, 2023. | Series: Creative Sports. A History of Hoops | Includes
    index. | Audience: Ages 8-12 | Audience: Grades 4-6 | Summary: "Middle
    grade basketball fans are introduced to the extraordinary history
    of NBA's Golden State Warriors with a photo-laden narrative of their
    greatest successes and losses"-- Provided by publisher.
Identifiers: LCCN 2022009470 (print) | LCCN 2022009471 (ebook) | ISBN
    9781640266261 (library binding) | ISBN 9781682771822 (paperback) | ISBN
    9781640007673 (ebook)
Subjects: LCSH: Golden State Warriors (Basketball team)--History--Juvenile
    literature.
Classification: LCC GV885.52.G64 W453 2023 (print) | LCC GV885.52.G64
    (ebook) | DDC 796.323/64097946--dc23/eng/20220224
LC record available at https://lccn.loc.gov/2022009470
LC ebook record available at https://lccn.loc.gov/2022009471

Nate Thurmond

CONTENTS

LEGENDS OF THE HARDWOOD

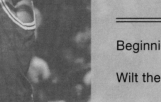

Stephen Curry

BEGINNING OF THE BATTLE

On October 30, 2009, rookie point guard Stephen Curry of the Golden State Warriors dribbled downcourt. It was just before halftime of a game against the Phoenix Suns. As he crossed the center line, he passed the ball to shooting guard Anthony Morrow. Morrow in turn passed to center Andris Biedrins who was on the right side of the basket. Curry curled back to the top of the key. He was wide open and Biedrins fed him the ball. Curry drained the shot. It was his first three-pointer in the National Basketball Association (NBA). TV broadcaster Gary Bender noted that Curry was "one of the [best] pure shooters you're ever going to see coming out of college." Hardly anyone else paid attention. The game continued.

It was a vastly different story on December 14, 2021. Curry and the Warriors were in New York. They faced the Knicks. At the 7:33 mark, Warriors small forward Andrew Wiggins passed the ball to Curry. He was just beyond the three-point line. As he had done more than 12 years earlier, Curry drained the shot. The arena erupted in a standing ovation. Officials halted play. It was Curry's 2,974th career three-pointer. That broke Ray Allen's long-standing record.

To make the feat even more remarkable, Curry broke Allen's record in 511 fewer games. That is the equivalent of about six full seasons. At that time, Curry was 33 years old. If he plays into his mid-30s or even later—as most greats usually do—he could put the record far out of reach for anyone else. "Everybody can root for him because he's not super athletically gifted, and he's a smaller guy," said

LEGENDS
OF THE HARDWOOD

JOE FULKS
POWER FORWARD
HEIGHT: 6-FOOT-5
WARRIORS SEASONS: 1946–54

Joe Fulks

"JUMPIN' JOE"

Joe Fulks' start to basketball was anything but
glamorous. He threw tin cans and balled-up rags
through hoops. A supportive coach gave him a
used ball. In that era, players almost always shot
at the basket with both feet on the floor. Fulks
discovered that leaving his feet and shooting in
mid-air gave him a huge advantage. Using his jump
shot, he became a high school and college star.
Later he became one of the first NBA superstars.
Fans loved the excitement he created whenever
he touched the ball. In 1949, he scored 63 points.
Some people called him "The Babe Ruth of
Basketball." "If it hadn't been for Joe," said NBA
Hall of Famer Paul Arizin, "I don't think basketball
would have made it those first few years."

Dirk Nowitzki, a former Dallas Mavericks superstar. NBA Commissioner Adam Silver added, "He has revolutionized the way the game is played and continues to leave fans in awe with his amazing artistry and extraordinary shooting ability."

Of course, this shooting ability didn't come about by accident. Curry almost always ends practice by shooting 100 three-pointers. Making 90 or more isn't unusual. This gives him confidence and helps him focus when he has one, two, or even three defenders trying to stop him.

The Warriors' story began in Philadelphia, 75 years before Curry's historic night, when businessman Peter Tyrrell founded the team in 1946. It was a member of the newly formed Basketball Association of America (BAA). The new team was called Warriors. Their 35–25 record was second in the league's Eastern Division. The Warriors faced the Chicago Stags in the Finals. Rookie forward Joe Fulks set the tone in the first game. He scored 37 points in an 84–70 win. He had led the league in scoring that season. In an era when most players had only one or two types of shots, Fulks "made one-handed shots, jump shots, right-handed [and] left-handed set shots from a distance, driving shots, hooks with his right or left hand," said coach Eddie Gottlieb. The Warriors won three of the next four games to claim the championship.

After the 1948–49 season, the BAA merged with the rival National Basketball League (NBL) to form the NBA. The Warriors made the playoffs in their first three seasons but fell in the first round each time. The bottom fell out in 1952–53. Despite a roster that included Fulks and season scoring leader center Neil Johnston, Philadelphia won just 12 games. That is the lowest win total in team history.

WILT THE STILT

Yet three seasons later, the Warriors were in the NBA Finals. Johnston and forward Paul Arizin were All-NBA selections. Rookie forward Tom Gola had been a high scorer in college. As a Warrior, he let his teammates do most of the scoring. He focused on defense, passing, and rebounding. The formula paid off. The Warriors surged to a 45–27 mark. They went on to beat the Fort Wayne Pistons, 4 games to 1, for the title.

In the 1959 NBA Draft, the Warriors took Wilt Chamberlain. He was called "Wilt the Stilt" because he stood 7-foot-1. He was a gifted athlete who ran the 100-yard dash in 10.9 seconds, put the shot 56 feet, and triple-jumped 50 feet even though he weighed 270 pounds. In his first game with the Warriors, he scored 43 points and grabbed 28 rebounds. The team went from 32 wins the previous season to 49. Chamberlain made a clean sweep of the major awards: NBA Rookie of the Year, NBA Most Valuable Player (MVP), and All-Star Game MVP.

He also began what is perhaps the most famous player rivalry in NBA history with center Bill Russell of the Boston Celtics. They faced off often during the regular season. Chamberlain almost always outscored Russell. But the Celtics had better teamwork. Philadelphia usually finished second to Boston in the division. It was the same story in the playoffs. The two teams played each other three times in the division finals between 1957–58 and 1961–62. The Celtics won all three. One factor was how the Celtics defended Chamberlain. "We went for his weakness," said Boston forward Tom Heinsohn. "We tried to send him to the foul line, and in doing that he took the most brutal pounding of any player ever. I hear people today talk about hard fouls. Half the fouls against him were hard fouls."

NEIL JOHNSTON
CENTER
HEIGHT: 6-FOOT-8
WARRIORS SEASONS:
1951–59

BAITING THE HOOK

Neil Johnston's father wanted him to play baseball. Johnston spent three years in the minor leagues. Then he developed arm problems. "I was a fastball pitcher without a fastball," he said. He turned to basketball. It was always his first love. He barely got off the bench in his first season. Johnston became a starter in 1952–53. He led the league in scoring. He did it again the following season. And the one after that. Johnston was especially noted for his sweeping hook shot. It was so accurate that he led the league in field goal percentage several times. He was on the All-NBA First Team for four years in row. Sadly, a knee injury cut his career short.

PHILADELPHIA VS. NEW YORK

MARCH 2, 1962

SCORING MACHINE

Wilt Chamberlain was on fire. He scored 41 points by halftime!
In the locker room, guard Guy Rodgers said, "Let's get the ball
to Dip [Chamberlain]. Let's see how many he can get." It didn't
take long to find out. Chamberlain scored 28 points in the third
quarter. The crowd screamed "Give it to Wilt! Give it to Wilt!" His
teammates responded. They passed up open shots to get the
ball to Chamberlain. After baskets, they fouled quickly to get
the ball back as soon as possible. With 46 seconds remaining,
Chamberlain sank a field goal. He had just scored 100 points!
In more than 60 years since then, no one has come close to
matching that total.

Chamberlain did have one small consolation. In a game in 1960, he pulled down 55 rebounds. That broke the record of 51 set by Russell. Chamberlain set several records in the 1961–62 season that will probably never be broken: 100 points in a single game, an average of 50.4 points per game, and an average of 48.5 minutes gameplay per game.

San Francisco-area radio and TV producer Franklin Mieuli bought the Warriors in 1962. He was a colorful character who wore a beard, jeans, Hawaiian shirts, and a Sherlock Holmes-style deerstalker hat. He moved the team to San Francisco, California following the 1961–62 season.

The Warriors' first season on the West Coast went south. The team struggled to a 31–49 mark. San Francisco drafted 6-foot-11 power forward/center Nate Thurmond to help take some pressure off Chamberlain. The Warriors improved to 48–32. They faced Boston in the NBA Finals. "That was a powerful, physical team," said Boston coach Arnold "Red" Auerbach. "Chamberlain and Thurmond were two of the best centers in the game." But Boston won the series, 4 games to 1.

Midway through the 1964–65 season, Chamberlain went back to Philadelphia to join the 76ers. The team had just moved there from Syracuse. That paved the way for Thurmond to emerge from Chamberlain's shadow. He set a still-standing NBA record of 18 rebounds in a quarter. But the Warriors won just 17 games.

Two years later, the Warriors met the 76ers in the NBA Finals. Chamberlain was the centerpiece of a 76ers team that had swept to an NBA-record 68 wins. The Warriors had a new star, forward Rick Barry. He had been NBA Rookie of the Year the previous season. Nicknamed the "Golden Gunner" for his blond hair, Barry averaged 40 points a game in the series. But the Warriors lost, 4 games to 2. Barry left the following season in a contract dispute. The Warriors still advanced to the Western Division finals. The Los Angeles Lakers swept them in four games.

GOLDEN STATE BECOMES TARNISHED

After several so-so seasons, the Warriors crossed San Francisco Bay to Oakland in 1971. They became the Golden State Warriors. "Golden State" is California's official nickname. Mieuli hoped the name change would broaden his team's appeal. The Warriors advanced to the conference finals in 1973. Once again, they had to face Chamberlain. He had been traded to the Lakers. The Lakers easily won the series, 4 games to 1.

Two years later, the Warriors swept through the conference playoffs. Center Clifford Ray anchored the defense. NBA Rookie of the Year forward Jamaal Wilkes provided scoring punch. So did Barry, who had rejoined the team. The Warriors faced the heavily favored Washington Bullets in the 1975 NBA Finals. For the first time in major sports history, the championship round had two black head coaches: Al Attles for the Warriors and the Bullets' K.C. Jones. Golden State swept the series, 4–0, to win their third title. "We cared about winning and did whatever we could to win," said Barry. "It was an atmosphere you'd like to see more professional teams have."

The Warriors went 59–23 the following season. It was the best record in team history. But they lost the Western Conference finals to Phoenix. They couldn't get past the conference semifinals in 1976–77. The Warriors then missed the playoffs nine straight seasons. The low point came in 1984–85. Golden State won just 22 games.

RICK BARRY
SMALL FORWARD
HEIGHT: 6-FOOT-7
WARRIORS SEASONS:
1965–67, 1972–78

NOT FAR FROM THE TREE

Rick Barry's five sons have all played professional hoops. The oldest, Richard "Scooter" Barry, had a 17-year career. He played in two American minor leagues, several European leagues, and even a season in Australia. Jon Barry played with eight teams in a 14-year NBA career. Brent Barry played 15 years in the NBA with six teams. In 2005, he and his dad became the second father-son duo to win an NBA championship as players. Drew Barry's seven-year career included several seasons in Europe and brief stints with three NBA teams. Barry's youngest son, Canyon, played in Europe and with the Iowa Wolves of the NBA G League.

GOLDEN STATE WARRIORS

Golden State hired George Karl as coach in 1986–87. The team earned a 42–40 record. It defeated the Utah Jazz in the first round of the playoffs. The Warriors faced the Lakers in the second round. Point/shooting guard Eric "Sleepy" Floyd established two NBA playoff records in one of the games. He scored 29 points in a single quarter and 39 in a half. The Warriors won, 129–121. But they won only one other game. Karl left the following year. He was angry because the team traded away most of its top scorers.

Karl's replacement, Don Nelson, put together an exciting, high-scoring young team. The Warriors made the playoffs fairly consistently. But they couldn't make it past the Western Conference semifinals. The team dropped to 26–56 in 1994–95. Nelson was fired.

RESTORING THE LUSTER

That was the start of one of the worst stretches of basketball in NBA history. Golden State failed to qualify for the playoffs for 12 years in a row. Three times the Warriors didn't even win 20 games. In two other seasons they won just 21. The playoff drought ended in 2006–07. The Warriors finished 42–40 and beat the top-seeded Dallas Mavericks in the first round of the playoffs. But Golden State struggled in the second round. The Utah Jazz defeated the Warriors, 4 games to 1. That set off another losing streak. This one lasted five seasons.

Eric "Sleepy" Floyd

Joe Barry Carroll

BUM DEALS

Two trades during the 1980 NBA Draft didn't work out well. The Warriors traded up-and-coming center Robert Parish and gave up their rights to power forward Kevin McHale. They drafted center Jeff Ruland and quickly traded him to the Washington Bullets. All three players made numerous All-Star Game appearances. Golden State received three players in return. Two of them made only minimal contributions and didn't last long. The third was 7-foot-0 center Joe Barry Carroll. He averaged more than 20 points a game for six seasons. He appeared in one All-Star Game. But many fans felt he could have done much more with his size and potential talent. They called him "Joe Barely Cares."

Help was on the way. Golden State made one of its best-ever draft decisions in 2009. It chose Steph Curry with the seventh overall pick. Even with Curry, the Warriors kept losing. But they kept making good draft decisions. They drafted shooting guard Klay Thompson in 2011 and forwards Harrison Barnes and Draymond Green the following year. These gifted young players helped the Warriors to a winning record in 2012–13. "It's inspiring to think of what we were able to accomplish this year and the foundation that has been laid," said coach Mark Jackson. They added to that foundation the following season when they traded for small forward/shooting guard Andre Iguodala. He was named to the NBA All-Defensive First Team that season. Golden State improved to 51 wins the next season. But they couldn't get out of the playoffs' first round.

Hardly anyone was prepared for what happened in 2014–15. The Warriors surged to a 67–15 record. They met superstar LeBron James and the heavily favored Cleveland Cavaliers in the Finals. The Cavs won two of the first three games. The Warriors came back to win three in a row. They took the championship. According to *New York Times* basketball writer John Branch, it was "as if the Warriors had caught the rest of the NBA off-guard with their small lineups and free-spirited style. Built from the outside in, dependent on speed and three-point shooting, the Warriors have none of the usual ballast that stabilizes traditional NBA powers."

Branch was referring to the "death lineup," featuring Green, Iguodala, Barnes, Thompson, and Curry. It was the start of a trend where a player's position and role had less importance in the overall scoring strategy. Golden State's lineup had a ton of offensive firepower and excelled on defense by taking advantage of the players' quickness. The key was Green. He often played center even though he was up to six inches shorter than his opponents. He made up for it with his physicality. He was named NBA Defensive Player of the Year in 2016–17.

Andre Iguodala

SOLID GOLD

Golden State exploded out of the gate in 2015–16. They won their first 24 games. That was the best start in any major professional league. The streak became the springboard for a 73–9 season. It broke the NBA record of 72 wins, set by the Chicago Bulls in 1995–96. Curry set an NBA record with 402 three-pointers that season. He became the first unanimous selection as the league's MVP.

But the Warriors couldn't get past the Cleveland Cavaliers. The Warriors became the first team to hold a 3–1 edge in the Finals and lose the series. The loss connected Golden State with the 2001 Seattle Mariners and 2007 New England Patriots. The three teams set all-time records for regular season wins but didn't win their respective league championships.

Golden State added superstar small forward/shooting guard Kevin Durant for the following season. He was a good addition. The Warriors met the Cavs in the Finals again. Once again, they took three of the first four games. There would be no Cleveland comeback this time. Durant scored 39 points as the Warriors won Game 5, clinching the championship.

The story was almost identical in 2017–18. The two teams met for the fourth straight time. The Warriors swept the series. Golden State hoped for a three-peat in 2018–19. It was not to be. The Toronto Raptors defeated the Warriors, 4 games to 2, in the Finals. Durant suffered a ruptured tendon in Game 5. Thompson tore up his knee in Game 6.

Kevin Durant

The series had a carryover effect into 2019–20. Thompson missed the entire season. Durant would have missed it as well, but he had chosen to join the Brooklyn Nets when he recovered. Curry suffered a broken hand and played in just five games. Iguodala was traded to Memphis. On top of everything else, the COVID-19 pandemic caused the season to be suspended for several months. The Warriors' 15–50 mark was the league's worst. Their season was over. So was the death lineup, at least for now.

Golden State rebounded to win 39 games the following season even though Thompson suffered a torn Achilles tendon before it started. Again, he missed the entire season. The Warriors narrowly missed the playoffs.

Golden State and Phoenix dueled for the Western Conference title and overall best record in the league in the early stages of the 2021–22 season. Thompson was fully recovered. But then the Warriors were plagued by a series of injuries. They finished third in the conference with a 53–29 record. Shooting guard Jordan Poole averaged more than 18 points a game. Small forward Andrew Wiggins added another 17.

The Warriors were healthy for the playoffs. They lost just four games in the first three rounds. As the team walked off the court after defeating Dallas in the last game of the Western Conference finals, Green shouted, "We're back!"

Draymond Green

STEPHEN CURRY
POINT GUARD
HEIGHT: 6-FOOT-3
WARRIORS SEASONS:
2009–PRESENT

KLAY THOMPSON
SHOOTING GUARD
HEIGHT: 6-FOOT-7
WARRIORS SEASONS:
2011–PRESENT

THE SPLASH BROTHERS

Steph Curry and Klay Thompson aren't related biologically, but fans call them "Splash Brothers." The two stars know how to "splash" the net, especially on three-pointers. The name is a play on "Bash Brothers," a nickname of 1980s Oakland A's power hitters Jose Canseco and Mark McGwire. In 2014–15, Curry and Thompson set an NBA record with their 525 combined three-point goals. They raised it to an almost unbelievable 678 the following season. The "brothers" have other things in common. Their dads, Dell Curry and Mychal Thompson, enjoyed long pro basketball careers. Their mothers, Sonya Curry and Julie Thompson, played college volleyball.

Golden State faced Boston in the 2022 NBA Finals. It was the Warriors' sixth Finals appearance in eight seasons but their first in three seasons. Boston won two of the first three games. The Celtics had home-court advantage for Game 4. Making things even more difficult for the Warriors, Curry had suffered a foot injury at the end of Game 3. He responded with what Thompson called the best game Curry had ever played in the Finals. He scored 43 points and had 10 rebounds as Golden State evened the series with a 107–97 victory. The Warriors won the next two games by double digit margins to take the title. As the final moments ticked away in Game 6, Curry hugged his father, former NBA standout Dell Curry, and cried. "It was overwhelming," Steph Curry said. "You know how much you went through to get back to this stage. It all paid off."

Apart from the disastrous 2019–20 season, it's hard to find a team with more success in the past decade than Golden State. Their four recent titles give them a total of seven, breaking a tie with the Chicago Bulls for third-most in NBA history. Only the Celtics and the Lakers, with 17 apiece, have more. Warriors fans expect them to add even more in the coming years.

Andrew Wiggins

INDEX

Jordan Poole